Janet Abramson

CORONA-COPEIA

Pandemic Poems 2020 – 2021

W0007111

AUSTIN MACAULEY PUBLISHERS™

LONDON • CAMBRIDGE • NEW YORK • SHARJAH

Ordering Information
Quantity sales: Special discounts are available on quantity purchases by corporations, associations, and others. For details, contact the publisher at the address below.

Publisher's Cataloging-in-Publication data
Abramson, Janet
Corona-Copeia

ISBN 9781638299004 (Paperback)
ISBN 9781638299011 (ePub e-book)

Library of Congress Control Number: 2023916320

www.austinmacauley.com/us

First Published 2023
Austin Macauley Publishers LLC
40 Wall Street, 33rd Floor, Suite 3302
New York, NY 10005
USA

mail-usa@austinmacauley.com
+1 (646) 5125767

I acknowledge the support of my daughter, Heather Krasna, for her encouragement and insight throughout the entire creative process.

Things to Do to Stop Thinking of Death

Eat, sleep, find an animal—vegetable—or mineral
to make sad sack desperate sex with,
drink smoothies mixed with gin or nibble marijuana edibles.
Hip and hop to hip hop, rock on out with Verdi and Rossini,
watch *Game of Thrones* for the 17th time,
wash your house including the attic,
boil your cabbage and stink up the neighborhood,
make 14 tons of sourdough bread and feed it all
to a Strasbourg goose, knit enough socks
for the United States Army guarding our oil everywhere.
Knit some mittens for three little kittens,
do yoga and twine your empty legs
around your empty head, bleach your hair—
your teeth—your skin, write the story
of your misbegotten cowardly life,
design a new mantra and set it up
to "Hallelujah," the Leonard Cohen tune
not the chorus by that good old white boy Handel.
Pop Melatonin by the ton
and CBD and mounds of magnesium, anything—
please God—to sleep more than your new normal

of four fitful hours if that.
Begin to read a book
then give it to a friend, leave it on her porch,
ring the doorbell, then run like a kid on Halloween.
Celebrate New Year's Eve and MLK,
St. Valentine's—St. Patrick's—Mother's Day,
The 4th of July and Labor Day although half the people…
haven't labored in half a year, Thanksgiving,
and Christmas and Easter.
And when you've Zoomed through
all of those, do Passover, Hannukah,
Kwanzaa, Diwali, Ramadan and Eid.
Celebrate everything for faiths and creeds
you have to look up on Wikipedia.
Order a closetful of clothes from LL Bean, then
send it all back or give it to the homeless family
in the home next door. Rescue a dog, a cat, a kid.
Remember the Maine and the Alamo,
lament the Titanic, the Ship of Fools
and all the little children everywhere suffering
without Mrs. Blindergast to teach them
how to wash their hands and their hearts and their young
fresh souls for exactly 20 seconds every time.
Sing like King David a new song. Wing it
while hang gliding—skating—sledding—meditating—
running—running—running—until at last
you run out of people—places—and things to run to.
Fling yourself face down—sobbing—
sobbing on the hard wood floor and relax into the hard wood
truth
that truly and cruelly and brutally you

like every other person who
has ever lived—
even Osiris and Lazarus and Jesus—
will die.

The Well-Tempered Soul

"…the center of the glass layer is under huge tension…Once a single crack gets through to the middle region, it's all over." Helen Czerski. "The Hidden Forces of Tempered Glass." Wall Street Journal, March 6–7, 2021, C–4.

The point is to stay on point,
To make enormous efforts to stand still.
Hold it together by force of will.
Deliberately design a gyroscope
spinning precisely en pointe
like a tiny Baryshnikov
balancing your core
to pull your insides tightly
intensely to your core,
your soul, altogether compressed,
by unbearable tension.
You bear it. You resist invisible forces,
exhaling lethal contagion.
You guard your well-tempered soul.
Not a single crack gets through
to you. You will never break.

Día V. Vita (Day Against Life)

The day begins at four-thirty or five.
The darkness weighs down—
Weighs down— down down—
the air—pushing down. Where
is the light, the first point
of it? The point of it all. There is
no good news. The disease—
remorseless— grinds like a glacier—
slowly pushing us— gnashing
our hearts in its teeth. The day
is long. A longing. The day is long
and the love in it—
is gone.

Disgraced

Rain-ravaged peonies, desecration
of the Queen of all Flowers,
elder sister of these antique roses
yesterday obscene in their lushness
brazen in buxom effusion,
white with magenta edges
nearing perfection. Then perfect.
Now shredded, splayed flat.
like over-used sled dogs
disgraced of their goal
to be for the briefest moment—
sublime.

A Master of Lost Things

"Be one of the people on whom nothing is lost."
— Henry James

But what if your everything is lost?
Swallowed by earth, wind, fire.
Lost in a sea of disease.
Forever so close you hear, taste,
inhale the scent of them on old clothes
found in a box stowed in the attic.
You hear them breathe beside you in bed.
They are felt on your skin, just glimpsed
in the eyes of a stranger or friend.
Each time a nanosecond of hope.
Over and over our everything
lives and dies and leaves.
And you are left, an artist,
a master of everything,
everything and everyone—
lost.

Because She Was Brown

(An ode to children caged at the Southern border)

Because she was brown,
we caged her.
Because she was brown,
she drank toilet water.
Brown toddler
walked from the equator.
Brown daughter
carried the water.
Brown sweet one
died in our sun.
Everyone, everywhere
watched her drown.

Hawks

Walking alone in epidemic-emptied park
following two sets of deer tracks
I climb the hill, panting, aiming
for the peak, and the silence ends abruptly.

A male hawk screams again and again
louder and louder. I scramble up panting,
stifled in a surgical mask, muffled in gloves.
The female hawk swoops, screaming
down from the tallest tree and the shrieking
pair spiral high above their hidden nest filled, I know,
with tiny gray and fluffy babies
clustered silent as the parents
dive one at a time, then as a pair,
screeching louder than I've ever heard before.

I gain the crest and spot the nest above.
The hawks take turns swooping down
to claw and tear the mask off of my face.
I ramp up the pace, the screaming swells,
the male divebombs, I race him
down the hill.

What does he know that I don't know
about doing what it takes—
screaming—
just to live?

Alone, Apart

(An homage to Ram Das—"Be here now.")

Look through your eyes.
See now the black swan, woodpecker, fawn.

Hear again for the first time
the hawk serenade the dawn.

Taste the ripeness of Queen Anne's lace root.
Be with me—heart on heart—
drifting—drifting—alone—
apart.

Anytime Soon

Our time is out of joint.
Think of it, how painful
a knobby bone when out of its joint.
It must be thrust, hard, back into place
by someone strong who knows how.

We wait. Beloveds seen
only on a screen, friends only voices,
unembraced, hands unheld,
backs unrubbed without the oil
of human kindness.

This loneliness kills us fast—
faster than a virus
flying like harpies, invisible.
Not killed.
Any time soon.

Dreaming of Danes

Hiking the trail I follow the tracks of the biggest boots I've ever seen.

The distance between each boot double the length of my stride.

Next to the boots are paw prints, enormous. If it were an ox, it would be Babe and the giant man called Paul.

What breed of dog? English Mastiff? Great Dane? Irish Wolfhound?

I decide it's a Dane and of course the man must be a Dane named Hamlet or Sven or Thorvald.

It's Hamlet and now I see him, immensely tall with mead-gold hair and chestnut beard. Eyes blue as a mile-deep fiord.

Parka with a hunting rifle slung over one shoulder.

His stride so relaxed and easy. I scuttle busily along, like a puffy-coated scarab beetle hitching a ride on a mastadon's leg.

I am already in love with him, ready to heat up the mead,
ready to throw a huge stack of mutton bones on the hearth
for the Great Dane dog I know for a fact is called Thor.

"Eppur Si Muove"
("And Yet It Moves")

So, it is said, said Galileo.
muttering his truth to power.
The Earth moves around the sun
defying beliefs of the ages.
He wanted two things but had to choose one—
his life or his truth. He chose life.

Like him, we are waiting and waiting
for life and truth
beautifully, at last, to coalesce.

Whole Moments, Alive

I visit two friends during pandemic
telling no one else as if it is a crime.
Wearing two masks entering and leaving
the house to be able to say
I did it. A bare-faced lie.

Inside the house we eat,
drink good wine, a lot of it,
devour intensely dark chocolate bars.

A skull with bat wings hovers above us.
We are almost normal, almost—
completely—
for whole moments—
alive.

Hades in Michigan

A Michigan winter is the ancient Greek
vision of Hades—cold, forever in shadow.
We try to hibernate like grizzlies,
living off the fatty salmon
feasts of the fall. But we fail.

We bustle about babbling,
making meaningless noises, fighting off
the whirling shades of our lost beloveds.

Their nearly visible faces, their empty eyes,
their reaching hands so close to ours,
almost touching cold bony fingertips
to our living ones. Ghostly icy lips
only an inch away, now half an inch,
breathless, caressing, stroking,
touching our ignorant lips.

Rafting

A quarantine is rafting like Huck and Jim
down a vast arterial river,
a flow so relaxed you don't know
you are fleeing
a million invisible demons.

You are the runaway slave
chased by dogs and men.
You are the orphan escaping your drunken father.

You bob in place on your raft becalmed,
waiting for the wind to rise,
for the river to run, for the whirlpool
you whirl in to open up
and the current to carry you
and finally, at last, to release you.

Euphoria!

A COVID shot—euphoria!
My shoulder hurts like hell.
Who cares? I love it! It is delicious.
If I were an aardvark, I'd flick it—
this yard-long tongue—
and lick it.

The Jewel in a Ring

I was once the jewel in a ring of love,
family circling, solid gold.
And I the diamond amidst
the man and children. Soldered.

Now I soldier on alone. Bedimmed.
Needing a chemical bath, a dip
in lemon juice, sunlight,
a good scrub in brittle snow.

Set me in a crown.
Display me in a shrine.
You can't bury a true jewel.
It is made to shine.

And a Virus Runs Through It

First wave in New York sends panic surging
all over the nation, the news spreading terror
of invisible droplets spraying the unmasked
innocents rafting on buses and subways
and ferryboats. They are free until they drown,
floating on their heedless way downtown.

The rest of us watch, smug, far away and secure.
What can you expect from an immigrant city
crammed with human flotsam washed up
onto our pristine, clean, white beaches?

The virus surges in a second wave, a third.
Even the tiniest islets of towns amidst
vast seas of grassland learn the truth—
we are all gasping without a raft
or a life vest. We are surrounded—marooned.

And a virus runs through it.

Sharp Sting of Truth

A COVID Haiku

Whatever doesn't kill you
makes you strong enough for when
some day—soon—it does.

What You Will

How can I quarantine?
I have no living quarters.

Can I be essential
and totally invisible?

Can I work from home
and also be homeless?

Teach me how
to tutor my children
in the broken-down car
that is our home.

Don't sugar-coat this pill.
It is EXACTLY what you will.

If Wishes Were Horses

We beggars would ride to get shots.
Our families and friends would still be alive.
There would be no evolution of covid.
The sand in the hourglass would rise up.

We would be connoisseurs of caresses,
laureates of lips, sommeliers of embraces.

We would meet to eat at every restaurant
in the world, from the sleaziest beaneries
in the Tenderloin to the Tour d'Argent in Paris.

Without a mask. Brazen. Fearless.
Braving an onslaught of vapor and virus,
defying an Antarctica of certain death.

A Perfect Time

This is a perfect time to find new love.
They meet in the park, bearing coffee
and donuts, his with sprinkles,
hers without. They find a bench
and toss crumbs to obstreperous
sparrows and squirrels. They tilt
their faces up to the sun, glancing
sideways briefly at each other,
telling the new person tales
of adventures, the top ten stories
of the buildings of their lives.

They stroll, trailing crumbs
to lead them back
to the subway
or cars
or bus.

At last they stop, smile, embrace.
Maybe this—yes—this is the moment
they will—almost—never regret.

What's Left Is Compelling

I am interested in happiness.
I find beauty worth contemplating.
Joy is a thing to fondle
like a warm egg straight
from the nest.

It is a sweet thing to see a moon
on clear nights, the third light
on my street. Each night a bit
of it is shaved or carved away
until the rind tremors on its edge.

Disappearance reveals the essence.

Always WHAT'S LEFT is compelling.
Always it is a CORE thing. A thing
that is entirely, unequivocally
itself.

Birds Sing in Darkness

Birds sing in darkness
half an hour before the dawn.
I see only darkness
and cannot justify their song.
How can they anticipate the light
amid a starless, moonless night?
Birds thrust forth their song
before they see the glory.
I insist on evidence before believing any story.
Yet birds persist in singing
long before the dawn.
There is a part of me that hopes
the singers are not wrong.

If I Leave in Spring

Will the hostas poke up noses
of pale green points when I'm gone?
Will peonies lift up red arm stems
with cupped finger petals
if I leave in Spring? Will the royal
purple irises stand fast amidst
The dandelions the day I turn
toward earth? Will the new grass roll
over me, a comforter at last,
when I pass?

Suburban Bacchanal

Strolling this proper suburb
with its edgy lawns, its competitive hedges,
its sideways glances at the yards
with delinquent dandelions
someone has hosted
Dionysian orgies, Bacchanalian debaucheries.
But none of them invited me.

I bag up their litter, snarling like a Salem witch.
There are Indica doobies in Zig Zag papers,
squat bottles of Maker's Mark and Stoli
and Jose Cuervo, an empty tube of lubricant,
a lovely lacy turquoise thong.
And sadly amidst the Big Mac wrappers,
condoms half-covered in mud. A used syringe.
Who are they, these rolling lovers,
these smokers and drinkers and junkies?
Are they the ones dropping blue masks
blowing around abandoned everywhere?
They are doing what my Hester Prynne
self would gladly, madly do.
But no one asked me to.

A Marquez Year: Haiku

Love in a time of COVID
feels like a hundred
years of seething solitude.

The Raptor

The vulture with a skull face
hovers, floats, rides on air.
A wing tip flutters
to brace his flight,
bending the cold wind
to his command.
Lording it above us, scaring us
into caring.

The Dinner Guest

Death is a guest at our table.
He's turning part of the group.
I set a fifth plate by mistake.
One of us silently signals to him,
daydreaming about the darkest Lover.
Only the thought of the business—
the burial plot, the ritual feast—
keeps us willing to fight.
We hold up our hands before our faces—
loose fists half turning into palms
opening toward the Lover
sitting silently—
waiting for his meal.

My Friend Died

My friend died at five on a dry morning.
The night before, I held her hand
and kissed it goodbye
as a subject salutes a queen
or as gentlemen greet a lady.
She was a lady and a queen
with a white crown and a white mouth.
I said, "You don't have to talk."
She said, "I don't want to."
So she slept all through the white night.
She lay asleep with wide open eyes
up to the very end.

My Vaccine Angel

Flailing like a trapped fly in the tattered web
railing at its nasty bugs,
its wobbling program, the evil screen
that shows you exactly how to register,
then waves goodbye, shutting you out.
A friend phones and offers a human hand—
"Let me walk you through it."
I, who never cry, feel salt tears.
She says "Left click, right click"
a dozen times and voila!
I have not just one but two appointments.
I send my Vaccine Angel a dozen roses,
a luscious chocolate mousse cake
and this poem handwritten
in India ink on antique Japanese paper.

Spiky Mullet: Don't Try This at Home

Three months into the shutdown.
Salons are shuttered. My pixie cut's wings
drooping disconsolately, I buy
electric clippers. How hard can it be?

Plug it in, attach a long-toothed comb,
rake it rakishly across my addled head.
Huge clumps float to the floor and
onto the vanity of vanities. The left side
is way too short. The right side
is a mile too long. Lop the long one.
Now it's too short and sticking out.
Match them up. Again and again.
The mania subsides into raggedy remorse.

I am the only senior citizen in all 50 states
of hysteria with a spiky mullet.

No to Thoreau

"Be it life or death, we crave only reality,"
wrote Henry David Thoreau.
But I say "No, Henry, No—
We are Christians in the Coliseum
dodging the king of beasts,
its relentless, tightening paws,
its jaws that scissor our throats.

We will fly to the moon and Mars,
spelunk into Plato's cave,
dive deep into an unmapped sea.

Anything, Henry, and everything—
to escape reality."

Our Faustian Bargain

We have sold our souls to the devil of denial,
labelled it kung fu flu
just to dance in a dive bar,
swim in a pool of pathogens,
bounce the ball against the wall
of NO, rip off the mask
at the Masque at Saint Vitus's Dance,
sing a psalm in the Love Thy Neighbor Church
as we sing a song that kills him.

Half a million bodies later,
half of us stare straight ahead
into the huge red eyes
of the Father of All Lies,
The Lord of Misrule,
The Fool in the Mirror,
the last and only one we see
as we drown in the Sea of Reality.

Spring Peepers

Spring peeper frogs sleep in baked mud
of the dried-up pond. The rains
revive them. Egg to tadpole
and then adult, they wake up
singing for a mate—

Love me— love me—love me—
Never leave me—never!

It is their fate, begin, beget and die.
It is the driest, hardest truth.
A seed of death erupts
each time there is a birth.

Lost Mallard

She flies just above my head—
zooms south like a fighter jet
over the tops
of forty-foot pines.
Disappears—

Reappears heading north
frantic solo rappelling
in the windless air
crying in despair—

"Where are you?
My drake? My sister? My home?
Why can't I find you?"

I see her completely.
And she sees me.

Two Human Sagas

Two great human sagas—
Someone leaves home,
a stranger comes to town.

Eden is our first home.
The stranger is a serpent.
We are evicted, forever fighting
to get back.

Life is our town.
Osiris and Lazarus and Jesus
leave town and come back home.

Over and over we need to hear it—

Ulysses and Achilles,
Moses and Noah and Jonah,
Huck and Jim
and Luke Skywalker,
E.T. and Scarlett O'Hara
and you.

We need to hear it
so we can bear it.

Fallen Tree

Huge fallen tree, root ball up
splayed for all to see
Like a knocked-out boxer sprawled.
How long until it softens, mushed
by rain and heat, dried by wind and cold
until it's gone?

Where does it go, the complex
mesh of fibers formed
into the annual rings,
rough bark, parched leaves,
abandoned nests?

The livingness that animals, birds,
people, even microbes
loved and lived among?

I have to believe the life
diffuses into ether,
I have to hold on to that other,
I have to absorb it
into my own rough bark,

my fibers, my leafy hair,
my own abandoned nest.

Meaning

The songs of the whales
are meaningless
except to the listening whales.

The dances of bees
mean nothing at all
except to balletic bees.

Raggedy V of the Canada geese
means vacancy
except to soaring geese.

The love in your beautiful
aquamarine gaze—
longed for, gone—
means not a thing to anyone.

Except to the whales,
to the bees,
to the geese,
and to me.

For all of us—
the songs, the dance, the V,
the glance—
means always, forever.
Everything.

Certainty

I demand certainty—
When precisely will this disaster end?

When the moon embraces the sun
and the seas of the world
shrink down to a pond.

When will I see your beautiful face?
Exactly the day and that day soon
when you hold my hand
and breathe my rasping breath.

When will I visit the Labyrinth
of the Minotaur in Crete,
The Great Barrier Reef,
or return like a salmon to the place of my birth?

And so beloved—
the big simple answer is—
it will not be today—
it will not be tomorrow—
That is the only certainty I know.

A World of Things

I used to be a world of things
and now I'm only one.

Call me widow, singleton,
I am an -un, a -non, an -ex,
a link in a golden chain
un-linked, a someone
now non-entity,
Excalibur ex-ed out
from its stone.

Floundering through a marsh
of solo stags bugling
their manly wares.
I stand waving the black flag
of a pirate in retreat.

Whale-Watching

Once I watched an adolescent whale
as he was watching me.
In our dance, I bent
across the bow. He rolled
on his side and presented
his enormous eye to me.
What did he see? How
did I seem? Not whale,
not fish, not worthy
of a song. Indifferent,
he sank slowly into
the eternal sea.
He left me to dive to infinity.

Truth

Children and saints tell the truth.
Unsaintly grownups lie for defense,
for offense, for a fence
around their mystery, a wall
preserving the treasure trove
of soul. No one can stand
the probing x-ray eyes
of the judges and they are all
judging, weighing your worth,
your value, how well or how ill
you fit inside their four-chambered
falling down shack.
Truthfully you are magnificent
domiciled within the limitless
palace of wonders
and universal beauty
of your soul.

Shoe

It's been there in the two-foot-deep hole
for two years. The small running shoe
pink and silver, all alone.
I see it every day except when
the snow drifts over it or
the mown grass shrouds it.

Where is its mate? When did she
lose it? Why? Did she hobble
crying all the way home, dragged
along by a fed-up mom?
But why did someone
carefully dig a two-foot hole and shove the shoe
toe down in the dirt?
Is this homage to a girl who died?
Who was she—NO! Not *was*.
Who *IS* she? Where?

And then today that shoe is gone.
As it appeared, it left me
looking down, two feet down
into the dark, now empty ground.

Want

I want everything as far as
eye and heart can see.
A lover of all perfections
who asks nothing at all from me.

A self-sufficient soul
always here right by my side.
Giving and receiving love
when I choose and when I deny.

Receptive, deceptive, elusive
with arms always open wide.
A lover of my rejections
which cannot be denied.

Plethora and Dearth

I have a plethora of days,
a dearth of embraces.

Weirdly, money in old age
after years and years of none.

More than enough of food
and drink,
never enough of lovingkindness.

A starvation of adventures,
an abundance of devices.

A banquet of irony,
a lean diet of joy.

A Glimpse of Ganesha

Once driving a usual route,
I stop at a light
and look around. A hill
behind a city fence
is covered with age-old grass.

There is a wind. The long fronds
of ancestral wheat grass
blow in concert side to side
like—what? Nothing I've ever seen.

Mongolian tundra of parched pasture,
Russian steppe of wild wheat,
vast South American pampas.

The wind blows the tall pale green
like dancers of India—
beautiful, arms swaying enacting.
Ganesha, the elephant god,
his magnificent generous trunk.

I have no phone, no camera,
nothing to save this beauty,
this perfection. Except my mind.
Unreliable, tenuous, only at best—
human.

Haikus

Chicory

Azure chicory.
Gnarled and scraggly stem and leaves.
A blossom or weed?

What It Is

Married fifty years,
plus one more. He died.
Still married to him.

Moth

Small white cabbage moth.
Wild grapes and chicory.
Here—not here—then gone.

Small Rain

Small, sweet misty rain
Greens the weedy patchy grass.
Here come the roses!

One Dead Tree

Long thin dead tree collapsed
on the power line.
The only living thing
a gold finch resting on the wire.

That tree could wreck us for miles around,
sending us back centuries.
No heat—no summer coolness—
No computers— phones—
Above all else—no light.

We would be annoyed—pacing
impatiently waiting to zoom
back into our accustomed
distance from the hard work
of wielding power.

Impatient—then edgy—then upset—
then panicked. The food!
Clean water! Artificial walls
of heat and coolness!

We feel our strangeness—
our actual bodies—
our meatiness and hairiness.
We smell a distant scent
of a dark and dripping cave.

Poison Ivy

Rose, Iris, Myrtle,
Marigold, Heather, Lily,
Willow, Ivy, Fern and Jasmine.

Girls are named for flowers.
But I am not a flower.

I am briar, chicory, poison hemlock,
Scottish thistle, barberry and all
the prickly, lethal, apparently benign
bristled, thorny weaponry
in the poisoner's apothecary.

Poison is a woman's weapon
it has been often said.

I can wait a long, long time
to choose exactly when and where
I will zero in on you
making sure this is the very last poem
that you have ever read.

Rammed Earth

(A Building Method Used Since Neolithic Times)

Take 60 tons of earth, add some water and lime,
or animal blood or nowadays concrete.
Stir and crush—crush and smash again—
Ram it with everything you've got.

Build a sea wall, a fortress
against a storm, a shelter
resisting all the forces
Nature brings to bear.

Join the invisible builders
whose rolling knolls we've climbed
for many millennia
back to the time the aurochs
and Neanderthals and wooly mammoths
roamed freely on the world.

It's About Time

White-haired man, unbuttoned shirt,
gold chains, driving
a '67 white Corvette, restored.
He's not restored, just old.
Next to him a young blonde girl
in a black halter top
and tight white shorts.
He has the slightly widened eyes
of someone watching the clock
run out.
She's totally relaxed, leaning
her light head back
against the cushion.
She has all the time in the world.

Building

You build with what you have.
In the Great Plains you dig
a hole, cut sod, live like a mole
under the treeless land.

In the Negev and the Sinai,
you gather rocks, dry-stack them,
use bundled palm fronds for a roof.

In northern woods, you cut logs,
notch them, use mud
to fill the chinks.

In the rain forest,
if you are a so-called pigmy,
every day you cut huge leaves,
weave them, nest with your family
curled securely around you.

And when your baby is born,
you say to the others—
"Look, children, see the new sister
that Mama has given us!"